"LAST WEEK, SOMEONE BROKE IN TO THE **MILLENNIUM BUILDING** — WHERE THE PLAYERS HAVE THEIR CHANGING ROOMS, A GYM, RESTAURANT AND SO ON.

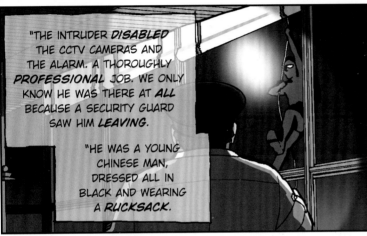

"THE INTRUDER **DISABLED** THE CCTV CAMERAS AND THE ALARM. A THOROUGHLY **PROFESSIONAL** JOB. WE ONLY KNOW HE WAS THERE AT **ALL** BECAUSE A SECURITY GUARD SAW HIM **LEAVING**.

"HE WAS A YOUNG CHINESE MAN, DRESSED ALL IN BLACK AND WEARING A **RUCKSACK**.

YOU SAID HE WAS A **PROFESSIONAL**. WHY IS THAT SO **STRANGE**?

IT ISN'T. BUT HE DIDN'T **TAKE** ANYTHING, EITHER! NOT A **SAUSAGE!**

"THE **POLICE** SEARCHED THE WHOLE CLUB WITH SNIFFER DOGS. THE ANTI-TERRORIST SQUAD WAS THERE FOR **THREE DAYS**. BUT THEY FOUND **NOTHING**. WHOEVER IT WAS JUST **VANISHED**."

MAYBE THE GUARD **DISTURBED** HIM BEFORE HE COULD GET HIS HANDS ON WHATEVER IT WAS HE WAS **AFTER**.

NO, HE WAS ALREADY **LEAVING** WHEN HE WAS SEEN.

NOW, ISN'T **THAT** STRANGE?

VERY STRANGE. BUT WHY ARE YOU *TELLING* ME THIS? WHY DO YOU WANT *ME* TO GO TO WIMBLEDON?

I BELIEVE SOMEONE INTENDS TO *SABOTAGE* THE TOURNAMENT.

THE *OTHER* COMMITTEE MEMBERS DON'T *BELIEVE* ME, BUT THEY DON'T WORK IN THE SAME *BUSINESS* AS YOU AND I.

IT JUST FEELS ALL *WRONG* TO ME.

WHY WOULD ANYONE *WANT* TO SABOTAGE WIMBLEDON?

IT'S *BIG BUSINESS*, ALEX. *MILLIONS* OF POUNDS ARE AT STAKE – SPONSORSHIPS, TV RIGHTS, MERCHANDISE, VIPs WHO PAY *THOUSANDS* FOR A TICKET TO THE FINAL...

SO YOU WANT *ME* TO GO AND SNOOP AROUND. I'VE ONLY EVER SEEN WIMBLEDON ON TV, SO I ADMIT I'D *LOVE* A TICKET FOR CENTRE COURT.

BUT I DON'T SEE HOW A DAY'S VISIT IS GOING TO *HELP*.

OH, IT *WOULDN'T*. I HAD MORE OF AN...

...EXTENDED STAY IN MIND.

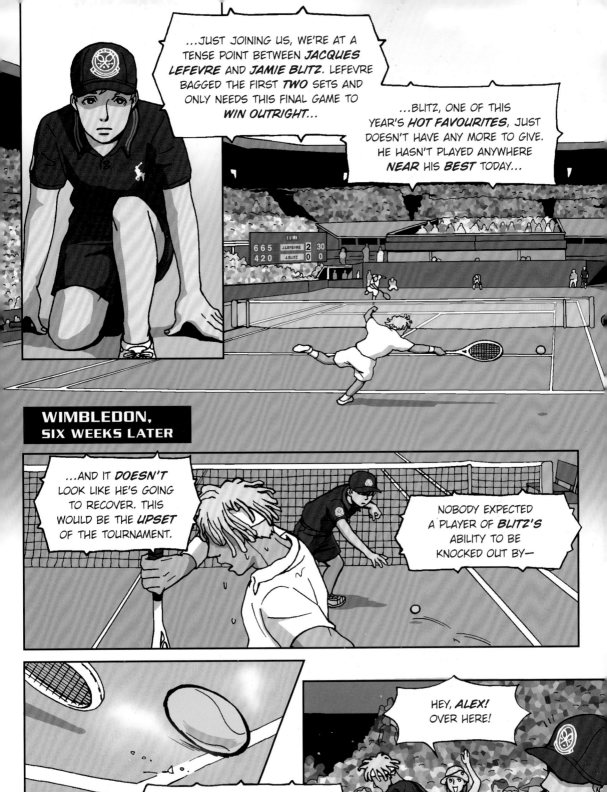

THAT WAS A REALLY *BAD* GAME. I DON'T KNOW WHAT WAS *WRONG* WITH BLITZ. HE SEEMED TO BE *SLEEPWALKING* HALF THE TIME.

IT *WAS* A BIT BORING, BUT AT LEAST LEFEVRE'S *CUTE*.

SABINA! HE'S SEVEN YEARS *OLDER* THAN YOU!

SORRY, MUM...

...

ARE YOU *ENJOYING* YOUR TIME AS A BALL BOY, ALEX?

YES, THANKS, MR PLEASURE. IT'S—

RIDER! I NEED SOMEONE FOR *STANDBY*. DO YOU MIND?

NO, SIR. JUST GIVE ME A *MINUTE*.

ALEX, *BEFORE* YOU RUN OFF...

WE'RE GOING ON HOLIDAY TO *CORNWALL* NEXT WEEK. DO YOU WANT TO COME *WITH* US? WE COULD GO *SURFING!*

ARE ... ARE YOU *SURE?*

WE'D *LOVE* TO HAVE YOU, ALEX. YOU CAN KEEP SABINA OUT OF *TROUBLE*.

THAT WOULD BE *GREAT!*

SORRY, I HAVE TO GO. I'LL CALL YOU *LATER!*

A *FAMILY HOLIDAY* ... I CAN'T IMAGINE WHAT THAT'S LIKE.

EVEN MY HOLIDAYS WITH *UNCLE IAN* DIDN'T REALLY FEEL LIKE A *FAMILY* THING.

AND SABINA'S PARENTS ARE REALLY *NICE*. THEY SEEM LIKE A REALLY *HAPPY* FAMILY...

RIDER!

GET A *MOVE* ON, BOY, THE UMPIRE HASN'T GOT ALL DAY!

YES, MR WALFOR! I'M COMING—

OH! SORRY!

THAT'LL TEACH ME TO *DAYDREAM* WHILE I'M SUPPOSED TO BE *WORKING* ... GET YOUR MIND ON THE *JOB*, ALEX!

WOW.

SWANKY PLACE!

IT'S THAT *GUARD* I BUMPED INTO AGAIN...

CRAWFORD SAID THE BURGLAR BROKE INTO THE *MILLENNIUM BUILDING*. MAYBE IF I TAKE A LOOK *AROUND* IT MIGHT HELP...

WAIT A MINUTE, HE WAS USING THE *PAYPHONE* IN THE *CAFÉ* A COUPLE OF DAYS AGO. WHY BOTHER, IF HE'S GOT A *MOBILE?*

...*OWEN BRYANT*. ANOTHER WORLD-CLASS PLAYER.

AND HE'S PLAYING *LEFEVRE* THIS AFTERNOON, TOO.

WHAT'S HE DOING, JUST *STANDING* THERE? HE KEEPS *STARING* AT...

HMMM.

NOW THE GUARD'S MAKING A *CALL* AFTER ALL ... BUT HE HASN'T *DIALLED* ANYTHING YET...

OH, MAYBE HE'S SENDING A *TEXT*. HE ONLY PRESSED *ONE BUTTON*, THOUGH...

...AND NOW HE'S *LEAVING* AGAIN! WHAT ON EARTH IS GOING *ON?!*

CRAWFORD WAS RIGHT, SOMETHING HERE IS JUST PLAIN *WRONG*.

I NEED TO TAKE A *LOOK* AT THAT PHONE.

OH! SORRY!

LIVE

BRYANT	6	6	4	2	0
LEFEVRE	4	7	6	5	15

...IN THE FOURTH SET OF *BRYANT VS LEFEVRE*, AND ONCE AGAIN WE MAY HAVE AN *EXTRAORDINARY* UPSET ON OUR HANDS.

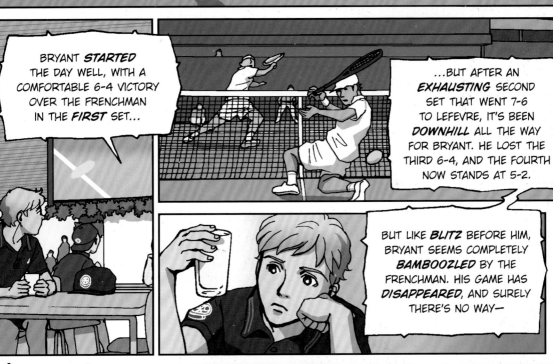

BRYANT *STARTED* THE DAY WELL, WITH A COMFORTABLE 6-4 VICTORY OVER THE FRENCHMAN IN THE *FIRST* SET...

...BUT AFTER AN *EXHAUSTING* SECOND SET THAT WENT 7-6 TO LEFEVRE, IT'S BEEN *DOWNHILL* ALL THE WAY FOR BRYANT. HE LOST THE THIRD 6-4, AND THE FOURTH NOW STANDS AT 5-2.

BUT LIKE *BLITZ* BEFORE HIM, BRYANT SEEMS COMPLETELY *BAMBOOZLED* BY THE FRENCHMAN. HIS GAME HAS *DISAPPEARED*, AND SURELY THERE'S NO WAY—

—NO, THERE *ISN'T!*

6	6
4	7

GAME, SET AND MATCH TO LEFEVRE, AND THAT MAKES IT 6-2.

ANOTHER SURPRISE KNOCKOUT!

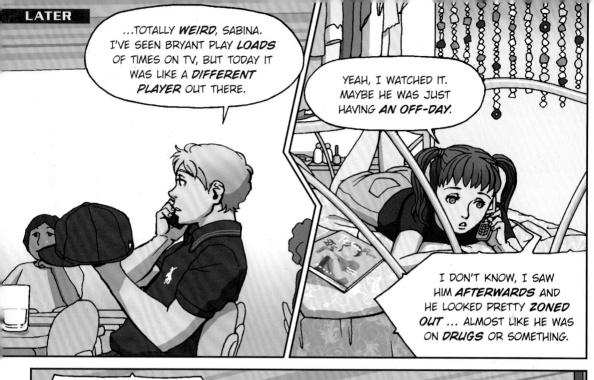

...TOTALLY *WEIRD*, SABINA. I'VE SEEN BRYANT PLAY *LOADS* OF TIMES ON TV, BUT TODAY IT WAS LIKE A *DIFFERENT PLAYER* OUT THERE.

YEAH, I WATCHED IT. MAYBE HE WAS JUST HAVING *AN OFF-DAY*.

I DON'T KNOW, I SAW HIM *AFTERWARDS* AND HE LOOKED PRETTY *ZONED OUT* ... ALMOST LIKE HE WAS ON *DRUGS* OR SOMETHING.

ARE YOU LOOKING FORWARD TO *CORNWALL?* DAD SAYS HE'LL *HIRE* A SURFBOARD FOR YOU IF YOU NEED ONE.

YEAH, THAT WOULD BE...

HOLD ON.

ALEX? ALEX, ARE YOU *THERE?*

SHHH. JUST A MINUTE...

THAT DOOR *DOESN'T* LEAD BACK TO THE COURTS ... WHERE'S HE *GOING?*

SAB, I'VE GOT TO GO. SORRY.

ALEX! WHAT'S GOING—

KLIK

HMPH. *BOYS!*

THESE ARE THE *SERVICE TUNNELS*, UNDER THE MAIN GROUNDS.

RESTRICTED AREA

THIS IS THE *"BUGGY ROUTE"*. BUT HE'S A SECURITY GUARD ... HE SHOULDN'T BE IN *HERE!*

ACTUALLY, NEITHER SHOULD *I...*

NOW, WHERE DID HE...

THIS IS *LIBRIUM*. NASTY LITTLE DRUG. A *SPOONFUL* WILL KNOCK YOU OUT FOR HOURS, BUT A COUPLE OF *DROPS* WILL JUST *CONFUSE* YOU. KNOCK YOU OFF *BALANCE*.

IT'S BUILT INTO THE *FILTER*, WITH A *VALVE* SYSTEM. *VERY* INGENIOUS.

SIR NORMAN, YOU REMEMBER I WAS WORRIED ABOUT THE *BREAK-IN* WE HAD.

NOT THAT AGAIN, CRAWFORD ... THEY DIDN'T *TAKE* ANYTHING! WE SEARCHED THE *ENTIRE CLUB!*

BUT WE DIDN'T EXAMINE THE *WATER DISPENSERS*. THEY WERE FIXING THEM *UP!* HERE, AND IN THE RESTAURANT ... PROBABLY *ALL OVER* THE BUILDING.

ALL ACTIVATED BY *REMOTE CONTROL*.

THAT'S RIGHT. THE DISPENSER FUNCTIONS NORMALLY UNTIL IT RECEIVES A *RADIO SIGNAL* FROM THAT *FAKE PHONE*.

THEN IT DISPENSES A *TINY* AMOUNT OF *LIBRIUM* INTO THE WATER. NOT ENOUGH TO SHOW UP IN A *BLOOD TEST*, BUT ENOUGH TO *RUIN* A PLAYER'S GAME.

PLAYERS LIKE *BLITZ* AND *BRYANT*.

IT'S *TRANSPARENT*, AND HAS VIRTUALLY *NO* TASTE. *NOBODY* WOULD NOTICE IT IN A CUP OF ICED WATER.

BUT I DON'T UNDERSTAND. WHAT WAS THE *POINT*?

THE GUARD ISN'T TALKING, BUT THE *TATTOO* ON HIS ARM INDICATES THAT HE IS – OR WAS – A MEMBER OF THE *BIG CIRCLE*.

BIG CIRCLE IS A *TRIAD*, SIR – A CHINESE *GANG*. HEAVILY INVOLVED IN DRUGS, VICE, PROSTITUTION ... AND *GAMBLING*. I BELIEVE THIS WAS A *GAMBLING SCAM*.

THAT FRENCH PLAYER, *LEFEVRE* ... HE STARTED THE TOURNAMENT WITH ODDS OF *THREE HUNDRED TO ONE AGAINST*!

EXACTLY. I'M SURE *HE* HAD NO IDEA WHAT WAS GOING ON, BUT IF HIS OPPONENTS WERE *DRUGGED* BEFORE EACH GAME ... THIS COULD HAVE GONE ALL THE WAY TO THE *FINAL*.

AND A HUNDRED THOUSAND POUNDS BET ON LEFEVRE AT THE START OF THE TOURNAMENT WOULD HAVE NETTED *THIRTY MILLION*...!

WHAT ARE WE GOING TO *DO*?

NOTHING.

WHAT?

IF ANYONE FOUND OUT IT WOULD BE A **NATIONAL SCANDAL**, AND **DISASTROUS** FOR OUR REPUTATION. WE'D HAVE TO RESTART THE **WHOLE TOURNAMENT** ALL OVER AGAIN.

CAN THIS ... **BOY** ... BE TRUSTED NOT TO TALK?

RELAX. **I** WON'T TELL ANYONE.

YOU DID A VERY GOOD **JOB**. STROKE OF **LUCK**, YOU SPOTTING THIS CHAP AND THEN **FOLLOWING** HIM.

YEAH, REALLY **LUCKY**.

I'M SURE WE CAN COME UP WITH A SUITABLE **REWARD** FOR HIM. COME **ALONG**, MY BOY.

NOT A **WORD**. LET THEM THINK YOU'RE JUST A BALL BOY ... ALTHOUGH I THINK YOU'LL HAVE TO STOP WORKING AT THE TOURNAMENT.

THAT'S OK...

I'VE GOT A DATE AT THE **BEACH**.

UH-OH...

SPLASH!

DID YOU *SEE* THAT? IT WAS *AWESOME!* WELL, APART FROM FALLING IN AT THE END, BUT...

ALEX...

...THERE'S SOMEONE TO *SEE* YOU.

HELLO, ALEX. SORRY TO INTERRUPT YOUR HOLIDAY.

YOU AGAIN, MR CRAWFORD! HOW DID YOU EVEN FIND ME?

WE HAVE WAYS, ALEX, YOU KNOW THAT.

I'M AFRAID *MR BLUNT* IS ON THE *WARPATH.* HE NEEDS TO SEE YOU *TODAY.*

ALEX RIDER

ANTHONY HOROWITZ

ANTONY JOHNSTON
KANAKO AND YUZURU

THE GRAPHIC NOVEL

WALKER

SKELETON KEY

YOU COULD HAVE GOT YOURSELF *KILLED.* I DON'T LIKE MY AGENTS TAKING *UNNECESSARY RISKS.*

I'M *NOT* ONE OF YOUR AGENTS.

CRAWFORD HAD *NO RIGHT* TO INVOLVE YOU IN THIS BUSINESS.

LIVERPOOL STREET, LONDON

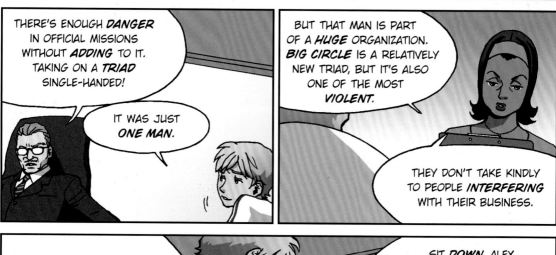

THERE'S ENOUGH *DANGER* IN OFFICIAL MISSIONS WITHOUT *ADDING* TO IT. TAKING ON A *TRIAD* SINGLE-HANDED!

IT WAS JUST *ONE MAN.*

BUT THAT MAN IS PART OF A *HUGE* ORGANIZATION. *BIG CIRCLE* IS A RELATIVELY NEW TRIAD, BUT IT'S ALSO ONE OF THE MOST *VIOLENT.*

THEY DON'T TAKE KINDLY TO PEOPLE *INTERFERING* WITH THEIR BUSINESS.

THANKS FOR THE *LECTURE.* I'LL BEAR IT IN MIND.

SIT *DOWN,* ALEX. YOU HAVE *NO IDEA* WHAT YOU'VE GOT YOURSELF INTO.

THE FACT IS, ALEX, YOU CAN'T GO *HOME*. YOU CAN'T GO TO *SCHOOL*. YOU CAN'T GO *ANYWHERE* ON YOUR OWN.

WE'VE ALREADY ARRANGED FOR *JACK STARBRIGHT* TO BE SENT *OUT* OF LONDON. WE CAN'T TAKE *ANY* CHANCES.

SO WHAT AM I MEANT TO *DO*?

WELL...

BY *COINCIDENCE*, WE HAD A REQUEST FOR YOUR SERVICES A FEW DAYS AGO.

THE AMERICAN *CIA* NEEDS A YOUNG PERSON FOR AN *OPERATION* THEY'RE MOUNTING.

YOU'VE ALWAYS TOLD ME TO KEEP EVERYTHING *SECRET*, BUT ALL THIS TIME YOU'VE BEEN *BRAGGING* ABOUT ME?!

ABSOLUTELY *NOT*.

BUT THINGS HAVE A WAY OF...

LEAKING...

IN OUR LINE OF WORK.

WE **TOLD** THEM YOU WEREN'T INTERESTED. A SCHOOLBOY, NOT A SPY, THAT'S WHAT **YOU** SAID.

BUT THIS TRIAD BUSINESS CHANGES **EVERYTHING**.

YOU HAVE TO **DISAPPEAR**, ALEX. YOU HAVE TO GO SOMEWHERE THE TRIAD WON'T EVEN **THINK** OF LOOKING FOR YOU.

SO YOU WANT TO SEND ME TO **AMERICA**?

CUBA, ACTUALLY. OR RATHER, AN ISLAND JUST A FEW MILES SOUTH.

CAYO ESQUELETO, IT'S CALLED, WHICH IS SPANISH FOR...

SKELETON KEY.

CORRECT. DESPITE ITS NAME, IT'S NOT DANGEROUS AT ALL.

IT'S A **TOURIST RESORT**, WITH LUXURY HOTELS, DIVING, SAILING AND SO ON.

THE CIA IS INTERESTED IN THIS MAN. **GENERAL ALEXEI SAROV**.

SAROV HAS A HUGE HOUSE ON THE NORTHERN TIP OF THE ISLAND. A **PALACE**, ALMOST.

SAROV WAS A COMMANDER IN THE RUSSIAN ARMY, BACK WHEN THE RUSSIANS WERE OUR **ENEMIES**, PART OF THE **SOVIET UNION**.

THAT ENDED IN 1989, WHEN THE **BERLIN WALL** CAME DOWN.

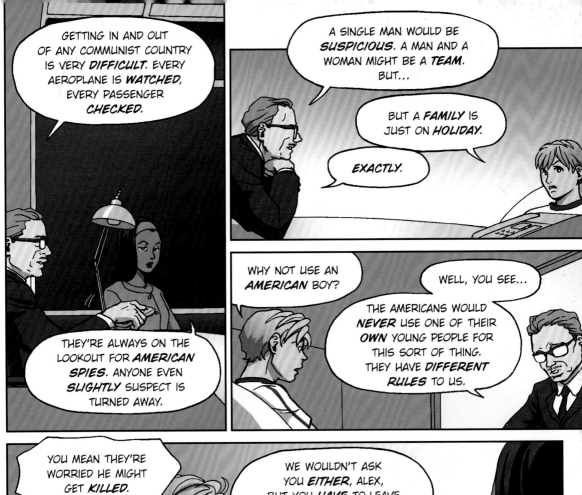

GETTING IN AND OUT OF ANY COMMUNIST COUNTRY IS VERY *DIFFICULT*. EVERY AEROPLANE IS *WATCHED*, EVERY PASSENGER *CHECKED*.

A SINGLE MAN WOULD BE *SUSPICIOUS*. A MAN AND A WOMAN MIGHT BE A *TEAM*. BUT...

BUT A *FAMILY* IS JUST ON *HOLIDAY*.

EXACTLY.

THEY'RE ALWAYS ON THE LOOKOUT FOR *AMERICAN* SPIES. ANYONE EVEN *SLIGHTLY* SUSPECT IS TURNED AWAY.

WHY NOT USE AN *AMERICAN* BOY?

WELL, YOU SEE...

THE AMERICANS WOULD *NEVER* USE ONE OF THEIR *OWN* YOUNG PEOPLE FOR THIS SORT OF THING. THEY HAVE *DIFFERENT* *RULES* TO US.

YOU MEAN THEY'RE WORRIED HE MIGHT GET *KILLED*.

WE WOULDN'T ASK YOU *EITHER*, ALEX, BUT YOU *HAVE* TO LEAVE THE COUNTRY, AND THE MISSION'S PERFECTLY SAFE.

THINK OF IT LIKE A *PAID HOLIDAY*. TWO WEEKS IN THE SUN.

I DON'T HAVE MUCH *CHOICE*, DO I?

THIS AFTERNOON. YOUR FLIGHT IS ALREADY BOOKED.

BUT FIRST, YOU SHOULD GO AND SEE *SMITHERS*.

SO WHEN DO YOU WANT ME TO *LEAVE?*

I'M BENDING THE **RULES** DOING THIS, BUT THERE ARE A **COUPLE** OF THINGS I'VE BEEN DEVELOPING FOR YOU, AND I DON'T SEE WHY YOU **SHOULDN'T** TAKE THEM NOW.

Whirrrrr

HERE ARE THE ITEMS YOU REQUESTED, MR SMITHERS.

THANK YOU, MISS PICKERING. TAKE THE **LIFT** OUT, PLEASE.

BUBBLEGUM?

CHEW FOR THIRTY SECONDS AND THE COMPOUND **REACTS** WITH YOUR SALIVA, MAKING IT **EXPAND**. AS IT EXPANDS, IT'LL **SHATTER** JUST ABOUT ANYTHING.

I CALL IT **BUBBLE 0-7!** HA!

PUT IT IN A **LOCK**, FOR EXAMPLE, AND IT'LL **CRACK OPEN**. OR THE BARREL OF A **GUN**.

NOW, THIS ONE IS CALLED THE **STRIKER**, AND I'M SURE YOU WON'T NEED IT. BUT HERE YOU GO.

MICHAEL OWEN?

BUT I SUPPORT **CHELSEA**.

OH. WELL, IT'S ONLY A **PROTOTYPE**, WE CAN DO A DIFFERENT PLAYER NEXT TIME. THE IMPORTANT THING IS THE **HEAD**.

NOW REMEMBER THIS, ALEX. TWIST THE HEAD *TWICE* CLOCKWISE, THEN *ONCE* ANTICLOCKWISE, TO *ARM* THE DEVICE.

IT *EXPLODES?*

ONLY A STUN BLAST. *FLASHBANG*, AS THEY SAY. TEN SECOND FUSE. IT WON'T *KILL*, BUT IT WILL *INCAPACITATE* THE OPPOSITION FOR A COUPLE OF MINUTES, GIVING YOU A CHANCE TO GET AWAY.

THANKS, MR SMITHERS. I FEEL BETTER NOT GOING IN *EMPTY-HANDED.*

WHRRR...

GOOD LUCK, ALEX. I HOPE YOU GET ON ALL RIGHT WITH THE CIA. THEY'RE NOT LIKE US *AT ALL*, YOU KNOW. HEAVEN KNOWS WHAT THEY'LL MAKE OF *YOU!*

YOU CAN TAKE MY *PRIVATE LIFT*, IF YOU'RE GOING DOWNSTAIRS.

UH...

NO, THANKS. I'LL TAKE THE STAIRS.

WHATEVER YOU SAY. JUST LOOK *AFTER* YOURSELF.

AND *DON'T* SWALLOW THE GUM!

NICE TO MEET YOU, ALEX.

HOW WAS THE *FLIGHT?* IT MUST HAVE BEEN *SCARY*, TRAVELLING ON YOUR OWN.

I HAD TO CLOSE MY EYES DURING *TAKE-OFF*, BUT I STOPPED *TREMBLING* WHEN WE GOT TO THIRTY-FIVE THOUSAND FEET.

YOU'RE *SCARED OF FLYING?!*

THIS IS *CRAZY!* YOU'RE PUTTING THIS KID INTO A *CIA OPERATION* AND HE'S—

BELINDA! TOM! CALM DOWN! ALEX WAS *JOKING.*

HE'S *BRITISH*, REMEMBER? DIFFERENT SENSE OF *HUMOUR.*

WELL, I *DIDN'T* FIND IT FUNNY. THIS WHOLE IDEA IS *CRAZY.*

YOU SAY THIS BOY HAS A *REPUTATION*, BUT HE'S STILL A *MINOR!* AND WHAT ABOUT THAT *ACCENT* OF HIS? NO-ONE WILL BELIEVE *HE'S* AMERICAN!

DAMMIT, WE'VE BEEN *THROUGH* THIS ... YOU *KNOW* HOW TOUGH THEIR SECURITY IS. WITH THE RUSSIAN PRESIDENT ON HIS WAY, IT'LL BE WORSE THAN *EVER.*

WITHOUT A *KID* YOU WON'T EVEN MAKE IT OUT THE OTHER SIDE OF *SANTIAGO AIRPORT!*

SO FIND AN **AMERICAN** KID.

AND TRAIN HIM UP TO ALEX'S LEVEL IN **TWO DAYS?** FORGET IT, TOM. NOW LET ME TELL YOU HOW IT'S GOING TO WORK.

YOU'LL ALL NEED **FAKE IDs.** IT'LL BE EASIER TO KEEP YOUR FIRST NAMES, SO IT'S **ALEX GARDINER** TRAVELLING WITH HIS PARENTS, **TOM** AND **BELINDA GARDINER.**

WHAT IF SOMEONE CHECKS **UP** ON US?

IT'S ALL BEEN **BACKSTOPPED,** SO EVERYTHING WILL CHECK OUT. WE HAVE PEOPLE UP IN **LA** WHO'LL SAY THEY'VE KNOWN YOU ALL YOUR **LIFE.**

NOW, TURNER AND TROY NEED TO GET INTO **CASA DE ORO** - THAT'S **"GOLDEN HOUSE"** - WHICH IS WHERE GENERAL SAROV LIVES.

YOU WANT TO KNOW WHAT HE'S DOING?

RIGHT. ONCE YOU'VE HELPED GET TURNER AND TROY **ONTO** THE ISLAND, YOU CAN KEEP OUT OF THEIR WAY. JUST STAY IN THE HOTEL AND ENJOY YOUR **VACATION.**

YOU HAVE **TWO DAYS** TILL YOU LEAVE, AND I WANT YOU TO SPEND ALL OF THAT TIME **TOGETHER**.

STARTING TOMORROW, THINK LIKE A **FAMILY**. BECAUSE THAT'S WHAT YOU'VE GOT TO BE.

SIR, I HAVE A MEETING WITH THE **SALESMAN** AT NOON TOMORROW! I DON'T THINK HE'S EXPECTING MY WIFE AND SON TO **JOIN** US.

AND I'M SUPPOSED TO BE HIS **BACKUP**.

WELL ... THE SALESMAN IS ALWAYS ON THE **WATER**, RIGHT? SO TOM, **YOU** GO ONTO THE BOAT WHILE ALEX AND BELINDA STAY ON DRY LAND.

WE'LL PICK YOU UP FROM YOUR HOTEL AT **TEN-THIRTY**, ALEX. DON'T BE **LATE**.

YAWN

OK.

I WANT TO SAY AGAIN HOW **GRATEFUL** I AM THAT YOU AGREED TO HELP US OUT.

I'M SURE **EVERYTHING** WILL WORK OUT **FINE**.

YEAH, RIGHT.

I ALWAYS KNEW THE PURCHASE AND DELIVERY OF NUCLEAR MATERIAL WOULD BE **DANGEROUS**. THE MEN IN THE AIRCRAFT THREATENED ME, AND PAID THE PRICE.

BUT, OF COURSE, THEY WERE WORKING FOR A **THIRD PARTY**.

BY NOW, THE **SALESMAN** WILL HAVE GUESSED WHAT HAPPENED TO HIS MESSENGERS. WHEN NO FURTHER PAYMENT ARRIVES FROM ME, HE MAY CARRY OUT HIS THREAT TO ALERT THE **AUTHORITIES**.

UNLIKELY, BUT A RISK I **CANNOT** AFFORD TO TAKE.

IN LESS THAN TWO WEEKS, THE BOMB WILL BE **DETONATED** AND THE WORLD WILL TAKE ON THE SHAPE I HAVE DECIDED TO GIVE IT. WE CANNOT TAKE ANY CHANCES.

CONRAD, YOU MUST GO TO **MIAMI**.

WHERR *IZH* HE?

HE OPERATES OUT OF A BOAT CALLED **MAYFAIR LADY**, USUALLY MOORED AT THE **BAYSIDE MARKETPLACE**. THE SALESMAN FEELS **SAFER** ON THE WATER.

PERSONALLY, I WILL FEEL SAFER WHEN HE IS **UNDERNEATH** IT.

YESH, GENERAHL.

SLEEP WELL, ALEX?

NOT REALLY. I WAS AWAKE *HOURS* BEFORE YOU CAME TO PICK ME UP.

ARE YOU READY TO ORDER BREAKFAST?

I'LL JUST HAVE *ORANGE JUICE* AND *TOAST.*

WHOLEMEAL OR GRANARY?

GRANARY, WITH BUTTER AND JAM...

HAHA! HE MEANS *JELLY!*

NO AMERICAN KID ASKS FOR *"JAM".*

YOU SLIP UP LIKE THAT AT SANTIAGO AIRPORT AND WE'LL BE IN JAIL - OR *WORSE* - BEFORE YOU CAN *BLINK!*

SORRY, I WASN'T THINKING.

HOW'S *LUCKY?*

...

OH, THE *DOG!*

HE'S FINE. HE'S BEING LOOKED AFTER BY *MRS BEACH,* OUR *NEIGHBOUR.*

TOO **SLOW.** IF YOU HAVE TO STOP AND THINK, THE ENEMY WILL **KNOW** YOU'RE LYING. YOU HAVE TO TALK ABOUT YOUR DOG AND NEIGHBOURS AS IF YOU'VE **KNOWN** THEM ALL YOUR **LIFE!**

I'M **SORRY.** I'M STILL **JETLAGGED,** THAT'S ALL.

SO HOW LONG HAVE YOU BEEN WITH THE **CIA?**

THAT'S CLASSIFIED INFORMATION.

WHO **IS** THE SALESMAN?

CLASSIFIED.

ALL RIGHT. IT'S PRETTY CLEAR YOU **DON'T** WANT TO WORK WITH ME, AND THAT'S **FINE,** BECAUSE I DON'T WANT TO WORK WITH **YOU.**

FOR WHAT IT'S WORTH, NOBODY WOULD **EVER** BELIEVE YOU'RE MY PARENTS, BECAUSE PARENTS WOULD NEVER **BEHAVE** LIKE YOU TWO!

ALEX...

FORGET IT! I'M GOING BACK TO **LONDON.** YOU CAN TELL BYRNE I DIDN'T LIKE THE **JELLY,** SO I WENT HOME FOR SOME **JAM!**

PLEASE, ALEX, SIT DOWN. YOU'RE **RIGHT,** WE WERE OUT OF LINE.

IT'S JUST GOING TO TAKE SOME **TIME.** WE DON'T **KNOW** YOU.

RIGHT. IF YOU GET **KILLED,** HOW'S THAT GONNA MAKE **US** FEEL?

I WAS TOLD THERE WASN'T ANY **DANGER**. ANYWAY, I CAN LOOK AFTER **MYSELF**.

I DON'T **BELIEVE** THAT.

WHATEVER.

THE SALESMAN IS A **CROOK**, BASED HERE IN MIAMI. MEXICAN GUY, A **NASTY** PIECE OF WORK.

AND HE DOES JUST WHAT HIS NAME **SAYS**. HE SELLS **ANYTHING** AND **EVERYTHING**.

DRUGS, WEAPONS, FALSE IDENTITIES, INFORMATION ... IF YOU NEED SOMETHING **ILLEGAL**, THE SALESMAN CAN **SUPPLY** IT.

AT A **PRICE**, OF COURSE.

I THOUGHT YOU WERE INVESTIGATING **SAROV**.

WE **ARE**. THE SALESMAN MAY HAVE **SOLD** SOMETHING TO SAROV. THAT'S THE **CONNECTION**.

WHAT DID SAROV BUY?

WE DON'T KNOW FOR SURE.

ALL WE KNOW IS THAT TWO OF THE SALESMAN'S **AGENTS** FLEW INTO SKELETON KEY RECENTLY AND **NEVER RETURNED**.

I'VE BEEN WORKING **UNDERCOVER** WITH HIM FOR A WHILE, BUYING **DRUGS**. TODAY JUST HAPPENS TO BE HIS **BIRTHDAY**, AND HE INVITED ME ON HIS BOAT.

SO YOU'RE GOING TO TRY AND FIND OUT WHAT HE SOLD SAROV.

WHICH BOAT IS **HIS**?

THAT ONE.

WOW.

TIME FOR ME TO GO.

I'LL STAY WITH THE *KID*.

IT'S ONLY A *TWENTY-MINUTE* MEETING. JUST EAT YOUR BREAKFAST AND WAIT HERE.

WHAT DO WE DO NOW?

WE *WAIT*.

SOMETHING'S WRONG.

WHAT?

WHAT D'YOU MEAN?

THE BOAT'S *LEAVING!*

BUT IT'S ONLY A TWENTY-MINUTE MEETING - TOM WASN'T MEANT TO *GO* ANYWHERE!

MAYBE HE CHANGED HIS *MIND.* MAYBE THE SALESMAN INVITED HIM ON A *CRUISE.*

NOT WITHOUT *ME.* NOT WITHOUT *COVER.* IT'S AGAINST COMPANY *PROCEDURE.* NO...

HIS COVER'S BEEN *BLOWN.*

YOU ARE A *FOOLISH* MAN. YOUR NAME IS *TOM TURNER.* YOU WORK FOR THE *CIA.*

AND I AM GOING TO *KILL* YOU.

YOU'RE *WRONG*...

I DON'T KNOW ... WHAT YOU'RE *TALKING* ABOUT.

I AM A VERY *SUCCESSFUL* MAN, MR TURNER. WHATEVER PEOPLE *WANT,* I *SUPPLY.* LIKE THIS *RARE WINE,* FOR EXAMPLE.

BUT I AM ALSO A *CAREFUL* MAN. I MADE CERTAIN ... *ENQUIRIES* ABOUT YOU. THE *CIA* WAS MENTIONED. AND SO YOU ARE HERE.

WHAT DO YOU ... WANT TO *KNOW?*

I WANT TO KNOW WHEN WE ARE *ONE HOUR* OUT OF MIAMI...

...BECAUSE *THAT* IS WHEN I WILL *SHOOT* YOU AND DUMP YOU OVER THE SIDE.

...AND I KNOW JUST THE THING.

TWO AGAINST ONE, PLUS ALL THESE OTHER GUARDS, AND THEY ALL HAVE *GUNS*. I NEED A *DIVERSION*...

MMMMF!!!

TOO ... HEAVY!

PETRO

NOTHING ELSE FOR IT...

RrrrriP

...I'LL HAVE TO MAKE A *FUSE* INSTEAD.

HOPE THIS DOESN'T BLOW THE WHOLE *BOAT* SKYHIGH...

PET'

ANOTHER *GLASS*, I THINK. YES.

BUT THEN I MUST *LEAVE* YOU. I HAVE *WORK* TO—

SEE WHAT IS HAPPENING! **QUICKLY!**

¡SE PRENDIÓ LA **GASOLINA!**

¡TRAIGAN UN EXTINTOR! **¡ÓRALE!**

TOM!

ARE YOU ALL RIGHT?

WHAT *HAPPENED?* I SAW THE BOAT *BLOW,* AND I THOUGHT YOU WERE...

IT WAS THE *KID!*

HE BLEW UP THE BOAT...

...AND *KILLED* THEM ALL IN THE PROCESS!

NO!

I *DIDN'T!*

NO! THERE WASN'T ENOUGH *PETROL* TO DO THAT ... THEY WERE STARTING TO GET THE FIRE UNDER *CONTROL!*

FOR *GOD'S SAKE,* KID! YOU THINK A *LIGHT FUSE* BLEW AND TOOK THE BOAT WITH IT?

YOU DID IT, ALEX. YOU SET THE GAS ALIGHT AND THAT'S WHAT *HAPPENED.*

YOU KILLED THEM *ALL.*

THIS IS THE FAMILY?

YES. WHEN WE **SEARCHED** THEIR LUGGAGE WE FOUND A **BOOKSTORE RECEIPT** - FROM **LANGLEY**, VIRGINIA.

WHERE THE **CIA** IS BASED.

EXACTLY. THEIR **IMMIGRATION FORMS** ARE ON THE WAY TO OUR **LABORATORY**, TO ANALYSE THEIR **FINGERPRINTS**.

SHALL I **ARREST** THEM **NOW**, JUST IN CASE?

NO ... NO, WE MUST BE **SURE**. WE CANNOT AFFORD TO SCARE AWAY **GENUINE** TOURISTS.

LET THEM GO FOR NOW.

VERY WELL. I WILL SEND THEIR **PICTURES** AND **FINGERPRINTS** TO THEIR HOTEL, THE POLICE...

AND OUR **SPECIAL FRIEND** IN **CASA DE ORO**.

WOW. THIS IS *IMPRESSIVE*.

CAN I GO FOR A *SWIM*?

SURE *THING*, HONEY! BUT YOU BE *CAREFUL!*

"SURE THING, HONEY…"

TROY SAID WE HAVE TO STAY *IN CHARACTER* IN CASE THE HOTEL'S *BUGGED*, BUT IT REALLY DOESN'T *SUIT* HER.

OH WELL. *ENJOY* IT WHILE I *CAN*, I GUESS!

I WONDER WHAT IT WOULD HAVE BEEN LIKE IF MY *REAL* MUM AND DAD HAD *LIVED*.

AN *ORDINARY* LIFE, WORRYING ABOUT SCHOOLWORK, EXAMS AND GIRLS ... NOT *SPIES* AND *EXPLODING BOATS*.

THEN AGAIN, I WOULDN'T BE SUNNING IT IN A *FIVE-STAR HOTEL*...

MOM? DAD?

NOT HERE ... TIME FOR *NINTENDO*, THEN.

BUT I WONDER...

TURNER *WAITED* TILL WE WERE BOARDING THE PLANE BEFORE HE GAVE ME THE *DS*. AND THEY *DIDN'T* WANT ME USING IT IN THE AIRPORT...

IS IT REALLY A *GADGET*, LIKE THE ONE *MI6* GAVE ME LAST YEAR?

Klik! Klik!

Press!

Jab!

NO ...
NOTHING.

OH, WELL. I SUPPOSE
NOT *EVERYTHING* IS
SPY STUFF...

Krkrkrkrkrkr!!!

kr...

*STRANGE ...
THE NOISE* STOPPED
*WHEN I PICKED IT
UP AGAIN...*

SOMETHING ON
THE *TABLE* MUST BE
SETTING IT *OFF!*

krkrkr kr kr kr kr krkr

OF COURSE.
THE ALARM CLOCK'S
HANDS ARE *LUMINOUS*, AND
LUMINOUS PAINT IS SLIGHTLY
RADIOACTIVE! THE DS
IS REALLY A *GEIGER
COUNTER...*

krkrkr kr kr krkr krkrkr

...THE CIA IS
LOOKING FOR A
NUCLEAR BOMB!

YAWN

WOW, I OVERSLEPT...

NEXT MORNING

...AND MY "PARENTS" COULDN'T EVEN BE BOTHERED TO WAKE ME UP.

GONE FOR A WALK THOUGHT YOU NEEDED A REST WE'LL CATCH UP WITH YOU LATER

MOM XXX

THE NINTENDO'S GONE...

THEY MUST HAVE SNUCK IN AND TAKEN IT DURING THE NIGHT.

"GONE FOR A WALK" ... YEAH, RIGHT. WITH A GEIGER COUNTER. WELL, I'M NOT WAITING HERE ALL DAY. I MAY AS WELL SEE SOME OF THIS FAMOUS TOURIST SPOT.

SO THIS IS **PUERTO MADRE**. "PLAZA DE FRATERNIDAD" ... **"BROTHERHOOD SQUARE"**.

YOU WANT **CIGARS?** BEST HAVANA CIGARS AT CHEAP, **CHEAP** PRICE!

HEY, **AMIGO!** I SELL YOU A **T-SHIRT!**

MUCHACHO! YOU BRING YOUR **PARENTS** TO MY **BAR**, EH?

NO, THANK YOU, I DON'T—

HEY!

THERE'S **TURNER** AND **TROY**. BUT WHO'S THAT **WITH** THEM?

SORRY, AMIGOS, NOT TODAY...

ALEX! WHAT ARE YOU *DOING* HERE? WE TOLD YOU TO STAY AT THE *HOTEL!*

YEAH, WELL, I *THOUGHT* THIS WAS MEANT TO BE A *FAMILY* HOLIDAY.

I *SEARCHED* THE HOTEL BEFORE I LEFT, BY THE WAY, BUT I COULDN'T FIND ANY *NUCLEAR BOMBS.*

!

KEEP YOUR VOICE *DOWN!*

YOU *LIED* TO ME. YOU'RE NOT *JUST* SPYING ON GENERAL SAROV, ARE YOU?

WHY DON'T YOU TELL ME WHAT THIS IS *REALLY* ABOUT?

...

ALL RIGHT. WE'LL TELL YOU WHAT WE **CAN**.

THAT'S AGAINST **ORDERS**!

WHAT **CHOICE** DO WE HAVE? HE OBVIOUSLY KNOWS ABOUT THE **NINTENDO**.

YOU MEAN THE **GEIGER COUNTER**.

WE DIDN'T **TELL** YOU BECAUSE WE DIDN'T WANT TO **FRIGHTEN** YOU.

OH, HOW **KIND**.

WE WERE **ORDERED** NOT TO!

BUT YOU'RE RIGHT. WE BELIEVE THERE'S A NUCLEAR DEVICE **HIDDEN** ON THIS ISLAND.

AND YOU THINK **SAROV** HAS IT?

WE **SHOULDN'T** BE TELLING HIM THIS. IT'S AGAINST **PROTOCOL**.

SHUT UP, TOM.

SOMETHING'S **HAPPENING** HERE. WHILE WE WERE INVESTIGATING THE **SALESMAN**, WE DISCOVERED HE'D GOT HIS HANDS ON A KILO OF **WEAPONS-GRADE URANIUM**, OUT OF EASTERN EUROPE.

AND THE PERSON HE **SOLD** IT TO...

...WAS GENERAL SAROV.

REMEMBER THOSE **ASSOCIATES** OF THE SALESMAN WHO FLEW IN HERE BUT NEVER **RETURNED**? WE THINK **THEY** DELIVERED IT.

SO SUDDENLY WE'VE GOT A MEETING BETWEEN A **GENERAL** FROM **OLD RUSSIA** AND THE **PRESIDENT** OF **NEW RUSSIA**...

...AND THE POSSIBILITY OF A **NUCLEAR WEAPON** IN THE PICTURE.

EVERYONE IN WASHINGTON IS **TERRIFIED**. TO BE HONEST, SO ARE WE.

WHY?

WHAT'S HE PLANNING TO **DO** WITH IT?

IF WE KNEW **THAT**, WE WOULDN'T **BE** HERE!

...I'M SORRY.

BUT NOW YOU SEE HOW **DANGEROUS** THIS MISSION IS. WE HAVE TO **BREAK INTO** CASA DE ORO AND LOOK AROUND.

...

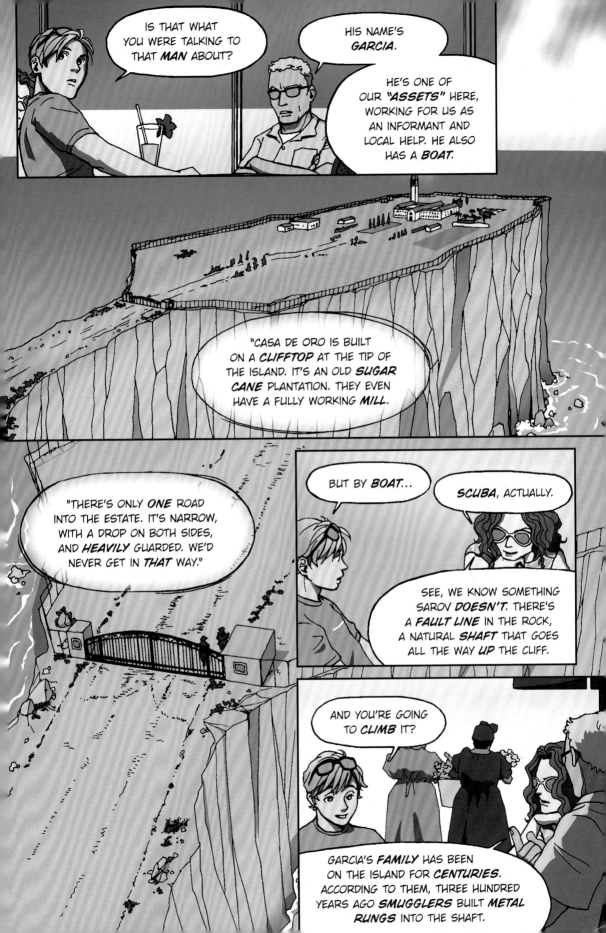

THAT LADDER RUNS UP FROM A **CAVE** AT THE BOTTOM OF THE CLIFF, AND COMES OUT IN THE **GARDEN**. **THAT'S** OUR WAY IN.

THEY CALL IT THE **DEVIL'S CHIMNEY**.

WHERE DOES **SCUBA DIVING** COME INTO IT?

THE WATER LEVEL'S **HIGHER** NOW, SO THE CAVE IS **UNDERWATER**. MOST PEOPLE HAVE **FORGOTTEN** IT EVER EXISTED.

SO YOU **SWIM** INTO THE CAVE, **CLIMB** THE DEVIL'S CHIMNEY, AND **SEARCH** THE ESTATE.

WHAT HAPPENS IF YOU **DO** FIND A BOMB?

NOT OUR **PROBLEM**. BY THEN, **OUR** WORK WILL BE DONE.

I SEE. IT'S A **GOOD** PLAN...

THANK YOU.

...SO I'M COMING **WITH** YOU.

!

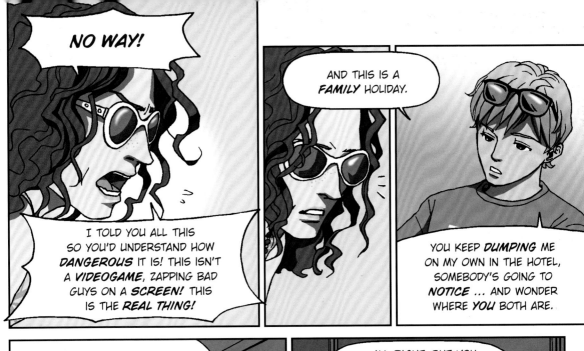

NO WAY!

AND THIS IS A *FAMILY* HOLIDAY.

I TOLD YOU ALL THIS SO YOU'D UNDERSTAND HOW *DANGEROUS* IT IS! THIS ISN'T A *VIDEOGAME*, ZAPPING BAD GUYS ON A *SCREEN!* THIS IS THE *REAL THING!*

YOU KEEP *DUMPING* ME ON MY OWN IN THE HOTEL, SOMEBODY'S GOING TO *NOTICE* ... AND WONDER WHERE *YOU* BOTH ARE.

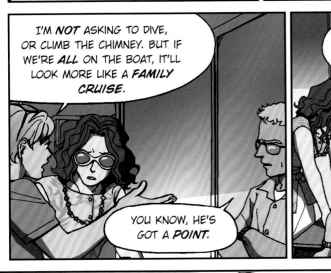

I'M *NOT* ASKING TO DIVE, OR CLIMB THE CHIMNEY. BUT IF WE'RE *ALL* ON THE BOAT, IT'LL LOOK MORE LIKE A *FAMILY CRUISE.*

YOU KNOW, HE'S GOT A *POINT.*

ALL RIGHT. BUT YOU STAY *OUT* OF OUR WAY, AND *IN* THE BOAT WITH GARCIA. THAT'S *FINAL.*

FINE. SO *WHEN* DO WE GO?

RIGHT NOW. WE'RE DOING IT *TONIGHT.*

WE'LL *DIVE* HERE AND *SWIM* UNDERWATER TO THE COAST.

WE'RE BEING *WATCHED*.

DOESN'T MATTER.

DIVE BOATS COME OUT HERE *ALL* THE TIME, EVEN THOUGH THEY *AREN'T* SUPPOSED TO.

THERE'S AN OLD *WRECK* AROUND HERE THAT PEOPLE LIKE TO SWIM AROUND. THE GUARDS ARE *USED* TO IT.

WE'LL BE *FINE*, PROVIDED WE DON'T DRAW *ATTENTION* TO OURSELVES.

WE'LL START WITH AN *EXPLORATORY* DIVE. TWENTY MINUTES, NO LONGER.

ALL WE NEED TO DO IS FIND THE *CAVE* AND CHECK THERE ARE NO *SECURITY DEVICES*.

THEN WE'LL COME BACK FOR THE *REST* OF OUR *EQUIPMENT*, CHANGE AIR TANKS AND GO *BACK* WHEN IT'S *DARK*.

YOU'RE NOT TAKING THE *NINTENDO*?

WON'T *NEED* IT UNTIL WE GET *BACK*.

YOU KNOW, I'M A QUALIFIED *DIVER*...

THE *HELL* WITH THAT!

YOU TALKED YOUR WAY ONTO THE *BOAT*, BUT YOU ARE *NOT* DIVING. JUST SIT TIGHT AND WAIT HERE.

YOU AMERICAN?

ENGLISH.

SO **WHY** YOU HERE?

I'VE BEEN ASKING MYSELF THE **SAME** QUESTION.

YOU KNOW **WHY** THEY DON'T LIKE YOU?

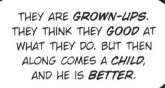

THEY ARE *GROWN-UPS*. THEY THINK THEY *GOOD* AT WHAT THEY DO. BUT THEN ALONG COMES A *CHILD*, AND HE IS *BETTER*.

WORSE, HE IS *ENGLISH!*

I DIDN'T *ASK* TO BE HERE.

BUT STILL YOU CAME.

THEY'VE BEEN GONE TOO *LONG*. THEY'LL RUN OUT OF *AIR* SOON.

MAYBE THEY ENTER *DEVIL'S CHIMNEY*. CLIMB *UP!*

NO. THAT WASN'T THE PLAN, *REMEMBER?*

DIDN'T THEY HAVE A *BACKUP* PLAN? WHAT DID THEY TELL *YOU* TO DO?

THEY TELL ME TO *WAIT*. SO I WAIT AN HOUR, TWO HOURS, I WAIT *ALL NIGHT*.

WELL, I'M *NOT* WAITING.

HAVE YOU GOT ANY MORE *SCUBA GEAR?*

YOU SHOULD NOT DIVE *ALONE*.

AS IF *YOU'RE* GOING TO COME WITH ME.

OF COURSE NOT. BUT TAKE *THIS*.

IN CASE, YOU KNOW?

THANKS. SEE YOU *SOON!*

Splash!

thud!

OUCH!

I'M OUT OF *PRACTICE* ... BUT NEVER MIND. I HAVE TO FIND THAT *CAVE*. AND QUICKLY, BEFORE IT'S *TOO DARK* TO SEE.

bzzzzzzzz!...

THE STALACTITES AND STALAGMITES ARE *FAKE*... THE WHOLE CAVE IS A *TRAP!*

AND IT EVEN HAS ITS OWN *DISPOSAL SYSTEM*. GROSS.

THERE MUST BE AN *INFRA-RED BEAM* TO ACTIVATE IT. THE SHARK *BROKE* THE BEAM...

AND I'LL BET *TURNER* AND *TROY* DID, TOO.

TIME TO GET *OUT* OF HERE. THIS WHOLE MISSION IS A *DISASTER!*

HAAAAAH!

MMMF!

NO, DON'T BOTHER *HELPING,* I'M FINE...

GARCIA, WE HAVE TO *GO.* TURNER AND TROY ARE *DEAD,* AND THE MISSION'S A *BUST.*

DO YOU *UNDERSTAND?* YOU HAVE TO TAKE ME *BACK* TO THE *HOTEL!*

GARCIA! ARE YOU LISTENING—

OH, NO...

NO, NO, *NO...*

YESH.

Whack!

CASA DE ORO

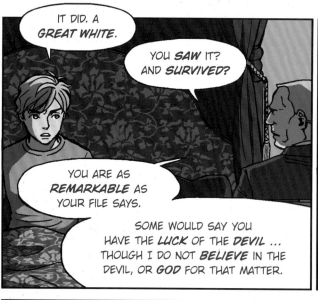

IT DID. A **GREAT WHITE**.

YOU **SAW** IT? AND **SURVIVED**?

YOU ARE AS **REMARKABLE** AS YOUR FILE SAYS.

SOME WOULD SAY YOU HAVE THE **LUCK** OF THE **DEVIL** ... THOUGH I DO NOT **BELIEVE** IN THE DEVIL, OR **GOD** FOR THAT MATTER.

BUT I BELIEVE IN **YOU**, ALEX RIDER. YOU ARE **QUITE** UNIQUE.

WHY AM I **HERE**? WHAT DO YOU **WANT** WITH ME?

YOU ARE HERE BECAUSE I **CANNOT** LET YOU **LEAVE**. CASA DE ORO IS YOUR **PRISON**, THOUGH I HOPE YOU WILL FIND IT **COMFORTABLE**. AS FOR WHAT I **WANT** WITH YOU...

IT IS **LATE**.

WE WILL TALK MORE **TOMORROW**.

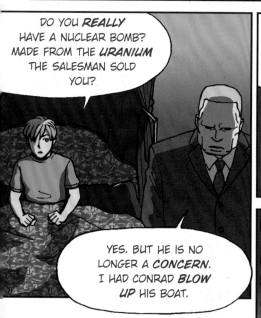

DO YOU **REALLY** HAVE A NUCLEAR BOMB? MADE FROM THE **URANIUM** THE SALESMAN SOLD YOU?

YES. BUT HE IS NO LONGER A **CONCERN**. I HAD CONRAD **BLOW UP** HIS BOAT.

CONRAD? SO IT **WASN'T** ME! I **KNEW** IT!

WHAT ARE YOU GOING TO **DO** WITH THE BOMB?

ARE YOU **AFRAID**?

I WILL **UNDO** THE DAMAGE OF THE LAST THIRTY YEARS! I WILL **GIVE** MY COUNTRY BACK ITS **PRIDE** AND POSITION ON THE **WORLD STAGE!**

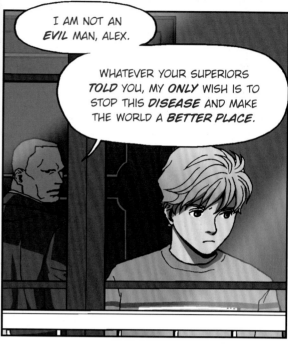

I AM NOT AN **EVIL** MAN, ALEX.

WHATEVER YOUR SUPERIORS **TOLD** YOU, MY **ONLY** WISH IS TO STOP THIS **DISEASE** AND MAKE THE WORLD A **BETTER PLACE.**

I HOPE YOU CAN **BELIEVE** THAT. IT MATTERS **VERY MUCH** TO ME THAT YOU SHOULD COME TO SEE THINGS **MY** WAY.

WE WILL **BREAKFAST** TOGETHER AT NINE A.M., THEN I WILL SHOW YOU THE **ESTATE.**

DO NOT TRY TO **ESCAPE.** THERE IS NO WAY **DOWN** TO THE COURTYARD, AND THIS DOOR WILL BE **LOCKED.**

MY PEOPLE MAY **WORRY** ABOUT ME.

FROM WHAT I KNOW OF **ALAN BLUNT** AND HIS COLLEAGUES, THAT IS **UNLIKELY**. BESIDES, BY THE TIME THEY BEGIN TO ASK **QUESTIONS**, IT WILL BE **TOO LATE**.

TOO LATE? FOR **WHAT**?

CASA DE ORO IS SURROUNDED BY AN **ELECTRIC FENCE**. THERE IS ONLY ONE **ENTRANCE**, AND IT IS **ALWAYS** GUARDED.

IF YOU **ATTEMPT** TO ESCAPE, YOU WILL BE **SHOT**, AND THAT IS NOT AT **ALL** WHAT I HAVE PLANNED.

TODAY YOU WILL MOVE TO **NEW QUARTERS**. I HAVE IMPORTANT **GUESTS** ARRIVING, AND IT WOULD BE BETTER FOR YOU TO HAVE YOUR **OWN SPACE**.

YOU ARE **STILL** WELCOME TO USE THE HOUSE, POOL, AND GROUNDS. BUT IF YOU CAUSE ME ANY **EMBARRASSMENT**, I WILL HAVE YOU **WHIPPED**.

NOW, **ENOUGH** OF THIS UNPLEASANTNESS. WE HAVE THE WHOLE **MORNING** TOGETHER.

CAN YOU RIDE A **HORSE**?

THIS WAS ONCE A SUGAR FARM, WORKED BY *SLAVES*. THERE WERE ALMOST A *MILLION* SLAVES IN CUBA AND CAYO ESQUELETO.

AT *FOUR-THIRTY* EVERY MORNING THEY WOULD RING A *BELL* UP THERE, FOR THE SLAVES TO START WORK. THEY ALL CAME FROM *WEST AFRICA*.

THEY WORKED HERE ... AND THEY *DIED* HERE.

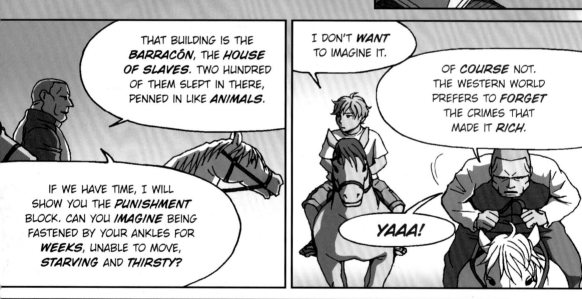

THAT BUILDING IS THE *BARRACÓN*, THE *HOUSE OF SLAVES*. TWO HUNDRED OF THEM SLEPT IN THERE, PENNED IN LIKE *ANIMALS*.

IF WE HAVE TIME, I WILL SHOW YOU THE *PUNISHMENT* BLOCK. CAN YOU *IMAGINE* BEING FASTENED BY YOUR ANKLES FOR *WEEKS*, UNABLE TO MOVE, *STARVING* AND *THIRSTY*?

I DON'T *WANT* TO IMAGINE IT.

OF *COURSE* NOT. THE WESTERN WORLD PREFERS TO *FORGET* THE CRIMES THAT MADE IT *RICH*.

YAAA!

HE *KILLED* TURNER AND TROY WITHOUT A *THOUGHT* ... BUT HE WANTS ME *ALIVE*.

WHY?

I WISH TO **TELL** YOU SOMETHING ABOUT MYSELF.

IN FACT, I WILL TELL YOU **MORE** THAN I HAVE TOLD **ANYONE** ELSE.

I WAS BORN DURING THE **SECOND WORLD WAR**, AS THE GERMANS ATTACKED MY COUNTRY. PERHAPS **THAT** IS WHY I HAVE ALWAYS BEEN A **PATRIOT**.

I ALWAYS BELIEVED MY **COUNTRY** COMES **FIRST**. I HAVE SPENT MUCH OF MY LIFE **SERVING** IN ITS **ARMY**.

I WAS MARRIED AT **THIRTY**. A YEAR LATER, MY WIFE GAVE ME SOMETHING I HAD ALWAYS WANTED. A **SON**.

HIS NAME WAS **VLADIMIR**. FROM THE FIRST **MOMENT** HE DREW BREATH, HE WAS THE BEST THING IN MY LIFE.

HE GREW INTO A **HANDSOME** BOY. NO FATHER COULD HAVE BEEN **PROUDER**. HE WAS TOP IN EVERY CLASS AT SCHOOL, AND A GREAT **ATHLETE**. ONE DAY HE MIGHT HAVE COMPETED AT **OLYMPIC** LEVEL.

BUT THAT WAS NOT TO BE.

I BELIEVED IT WAS **RIGHT** FOR VLADIMIR TO SERVE HIS COUNTRY, AS I HAD, AND JOIN THE **ARMY**. HIS MOTHER **DISAGREED**, AND THAT DISAGREEMENT **ENDED** OUR MARRIAGE.

HE WENT TO *AFGHANISTAN*, WHERE WE WERE FIGHTING A HARD, *DIFFICULT* WAR.

YOU ASKED HER TO *LEAVE?*

I *ORDERED* HER TO!

VLADIMIR *JOINED* THE ARMY. HE WAS JUST *SIXTEEN* YEARS OLD.

THREE WEEKS INTO HIS TOUR, A *SNIPER* SHOT HIM AND HE *DIED.*

THE WAR *ENDED* A YEAR LATER. OUR *COWARDLY* GOVERNMENT LOST THE *SPIRIT* TO FIGHT. IT HAD ALL BEEN FOR *NOTHING!*

AND THERE IS *NOTHING* MORE TERRIBLE THAN FOR A FATHER TO *LOSE* HIS SON.

...

BUT THEN I MET *YOU.*

ME?

I DON'T UNDERSTAND...

YOU HAVE SO MUCH IN *COMMON*, ALEX. JUST FOURTEEN, AND *ALREADY* SERVING YOUR COUNTRY! HOW *RARE* TO FIND A YOUNG PERSON *WILLING* TO FIGHT FOR THEIR BELIEFS!

I WOULDN'T GO *THAT* FAR...

'NIGHT, CONRAD! I'LL **CALL** YOU IF I NEED ANYTHING!

FSSh!

FLOODLIGHTS?

OF COURSE. SAROV'S **VISITORS** HAVE ARRIVED.

AND THERE'S THE **RUSSIAN PRESIDENT.**

WHATEVER SAROV'S UP TO ... IT'S **BEGUN.**

NEXT MORNING

WHO ARE YOU?

SERÉ TU *ESCOLTA* EL DÍA DE HOY.

¡DESPIERTA, POR FAVOR!

"ESCORT"? *FOLLOWING* ME SO I DON'T TRY TO *ESCAPE*, MORE LIKE. WHAT'S YOUR NAME?

¿COMO SE LLAMA USTED?

JUAN. ¿QUIERES DESAYUNAR?

BREAKFAST? NO ... NO, TAKE ME TO THE *STABLES*. I WANT TO GO RIDING AGAIN. *MONTAR A CABALLO*.

ACTUALLY I WANT TO CHECK OUT THAT *ELECTRIC FENCE*, SEE IF THERE'S A TREE I CAN USE TO CLIMB *OVER* IT...

YAAA!

WELL, SO MUCH FOR THAT IDEA. NOT A TREE IN SIGHT.

PELIGRO!

LATER

AND THE DEAD BIRD TELLS ME THOSE "DANGER!" SIGNS OBVIOUSLY AREN'T KIDDING. THAT'S ONE ESCAPE ROUTE I CAN FORGET ABOUT.

WHAT ABOUT THE ENTRANCE GATE? TURNER SAID THERE WAS ONLY ONE ROAD INTO THE ESTATE...

THREE ARMED GUARDS, AND THE FENCE GOES ALL THE WAY UP TO THE BARRIER. DOESN'T LOOK PROMISING—

Beep Beep

MALCHIK, PODVINSYA!

HMMM.

COME ON, JUAN. LET'S GO HAVE THAT *BREAKFAST.*

SOON

Splash!

GIGGLE

HELLO, WHAT'S GOING ON AT THE *POOL?*

GOOD MORNING, ALEX! COME HERE!

ALLOW ME TO INTRODUCE MY OLD FRIEND, **BORIS KIRIYENKO ... THE PRESIDENT OF RUSSIA.**

BORIS, **THIS** IS THE BOY I WAS TELLING YOU ABOUT.

IT IS A **PLEASURE.**

TY BIL PRAV, ON POKHOZJ NA VLADIMIRA.

SORRY, WHAT?

YOU **REMIND** HIM OF MY SON.

WOULD YOU LIKE A **SWIM**, ALEX? TO COOL YOU DOWN AFTER **RIDING?**

NO THANKS. **UNUSUAL LIFEGUARDS** YOU HAVE THERE.

SOME **COMPANY** FOR OUR GUEST. AFTER ALL, BORIS IS ON **HOLIDAY.**

UNFORTUNATELY, WE STILL HAVE **WORK** TO DO. A LOCAL **TV STATION** HAS REQUESTED AN **INTERVIEW** WITH OUR DISTINGUISHED VISITOR, AND BORIS HAS **AGREED.**

AH, *HERE* THEY ARE NOW!

YOU CAN HAVE THE *POOL* TO YOURSELF, ALEX. WE'RE GOING INTO *SANTIAGO* AFTER LUNCH, BUT I HOPE YOU'LL JOIN US FOR *DINNER*. THE CHEF HAS PLANNED A VERY *SPECIAL* MAIN COURSE.

POYEZHAI, BORIS. TAM BUDET BEZUPRECHNO.

GIGGLE

INTO *SANTIAGO*, EH? THAT COULD BE MY *CHANCE*...

...IF I CAN DO SOMETHING ABOUT *JUAN*, THAT IS.

SANTIAGO AFTER LUNCH ... HOPE THEY TAKE *ALL* OF THE LIMOS.

ENTERVYU S PRIZIDENTOM PROSHLO HOROSHO, YA DUMAYU.

!

NEED TO FIND SOMEWHERE TO *HIDE...*

A-HA!

BRRRR, SERIOUS AIR-CONDITIONING! WHICH PART OF THE HOUSE IS *THIS...*?

...OH. I HAVEN'T BEEN IN *HERE* YET!

SOME KIND OF *EDITING SUITE*, LIKE A *TV STUDIO* ... THEY'RE WATCHING THE WHOLE *HOUSE!*

BUT THOSE ARE *RECORDINGS* OF STUFF THAT HAPPENED *EARLIER* ... WHAT ARE THEY *DOING* IN HERE?

NO *TIME* TO THINK ABOUT THAT NOW. I HAVE TO GET *OUT* AND CONTACT THE *CIA!*

THE *GUARDS* HAVE GONE, BUT LUNCH WILL BE OVER SOON. IT'S *NOW* OR *NEVER*.

I JUST HOPE ONE OF THEM IS *OPEN*...

KLIK

...BINGO!

AND NOW ... I *WAIT*.

PHEW!
HOTTER IN HERE THAN I EXPECTED. I HOPE THEY DON'T TAKE TOO LONG.
SOMEONE'S COMING, BUT I CAN'T MAKE OUT WHAT THEY'RE SAYING...
Whump
YES! I PICKED A GOOD CAR...
Vrrrrrrm...
...AND NOW WE'RE MOVING. SO FAR, SO GOOD.
STOPPED AGAIN. MUST BE AT THE GATE.
PLEASE DON'T OPEN THE BOOT, YOU DIDN'T CHECK IT ON THAT CAR THIS MORNING...
...MOVING AGAIN! I WONDER HOW FAR IT IS TO SANTIAGO? I'LL HAVE TO LISTEN OUT FOR WHEN WE ARRIVE.
THEN I CAN USE THE CHEWING GUM SMITHERS GAVE ME TO BLOW OPEN THE BOOT...
WAIT, WHAT'S HAPPENING?
WE'VE STOPPED AGAIN!

IT IS A VERY SOPHISTICATED *SENSOR*. IT DETECTS THE *HUMAN HEARTBEAT*.

Ba-dum ...

Ba-dum ...

Ba-dum ...

EVERY CAR IS *SCANNED* AT THE BARRIER. WHEN THE GUARD HEARD *ONE MORE* HEARTBEAT THAN HE *SHOULD* HAVE, HE KNEW SOMETHING WAS *WRONG*.

Ba-dum ...

Ba-dum ...

DO YOU NOT *REMEMBER* WHAT I TOLD YOU? THAT IF YOU TRIED TO *ESCAPE*, YOU COULD BE *SHOT*?

CONRAD *VERY MUCH* WISHES TO SHOOT YOU. HE BELIEVES I AM A *FOOL* TO KEEP YOU AS MY GUEST.

HE IS *RIGHT*.

AFTER *ALL* I HAVE OFFERED YOU, YOU MAKE AN *ENEMY* OF ME. I WANT YOU TO BE MY *SON* ... BUT YOU FORCE ME TO *DESTROY* YOU.

Ba-dum ...a-dum

...um Ba... -dum

THIS IS FOR ME A NIGHT OF GREAT *SIGNIFICANCE*. WHAT CAN I TELL YOU ABOUT *BORIS NIKITA KIRIYENKO?* MY CLOSEST AND DEAREST FRIEND FOR *FIFTY YEARS!*

I STILL REMEMBER HIM AS A CHILD WHO *TEASED ANIMALS*, WHO *CRIED* WHEN THERE WAS A FIGHT, AND *NEVER* TOLD THE TRUTH.

IT IS HARD TO *BELIEVE* THIS IS THE SAME MAN ENTRUSTED WITH THE *PRIVILEGE*, THE SACRED *HONOUR*, OF LEADING OUR GREAT COUNTRY IN THESE *DIFFICULT* TIMES.

WELL, BORIS HAS COME HERE FOR A *HOLIDAY*. I'M SURE HE *NEEDS* ONE AFTER SO MUCH WORK. AND *THAT* IS THE TOAST I WISH TO MAKE TONIGHT.

TO BORIS'S HOLIDAY! I HOPE IT WILL BE LONGER AND MORE MEMORABLE THAN HE *EVER* EXPECTED.

OSTOROZJNO!

THAT'S THE *BOMB* ... ISN'T IT?

GET IN. WE MUST *NOT* WASTE TIME.

...

COME. WE ARE TO TAKE OFF *IMMEDIATELY*.

I HAVE DECIDED TO **ARRANGE** THAT ACCIDENT.

IF ONE OF THE SUBMARINES **BLEW UP**, IT WOULD BE A **CATASTROPHE**. A HUGE NUMBER OF RUSSIANS IN THE KOLA PENINSULA AND THE NORTH, AS WELL AS MANY MORE IN NORWAY AND FINLAND, WOULD **DIE** IMMEDIATELY.

THE **FALLOUT** WOULD REACH EUROPE, MAKING LONDON **UNINHABITABLE** FOR MANY YEARS. AND THOUSANDS **MORE** WOULD FALL ILL AND DIE SLOW, PAINFUL DEATHS.

SO WHY **DO** IT? WHAT WILL IT **ACHIEVE**?

I AM GIVING THE WORLD A **WAKE-UP CALL**.

TOMORROW NIGHT I WILL PLACE THE **BOMB** AMONGST THE SUBMARINES.

THE **CODES** REQUIRED TO DETONATE THE BOMB ARE ENCODED ON THIS **KEY CARD**. I WILL **INSERT** IT INTO THE CASING, THEN LEAVE.

AT THE TIME OF THE **EXPLOSION** I WILL BE ON MY WAY TO **MOSCOW**.

BUT THE **SHOCKWAVE** WILL BE FELT AROUND THE **WHOLE WORLD**!

IMAGINE THE *OUTRAGE* IT WILL CREATE! THEY WILL ASSUME ONE OF THE *SUBMARINES* FINALLY *COLLAPSED*. NOBODY WILL SUSPECT THE *TRUTH*.

YES, THEY *WILL!* THE CIA *KNOWS* YOU BOUGHT URANIUM! THEY'LL FIND OUT THEIR AGENTS ARE *DEAD*—

NOBODY WILL *BELIEVE* THE CIA. NOBODY EVER *DOES*. ANYWAY, IT WILL BE TOO *LATE*.

INSTEAD, THE WORLD WILL *UNITE* TO *CONDEMN RUSSIA* OVER THE DISASTER. WE WILL BE *HATED*. THE RUSSIAN PEOPLE WILL BE *ASHAMED*.

"IF ONLY WE HAD BEEN *LESS* CARELESS, *LESS* POOR, *LESS* CORRUPT. IF ONLY WE WERE STILL THE SUPERPOWER WE HAD *ONCE* BEEN..."

EVERYONE WILL LOOK TO *BORIS KIRIYENKO*, THE RUSSIAN PRESIDENT, FOR *LEADERSHIP*. AND WHAT WILL THEY *SEE?*

THE *EDITING SUITE!*

YOU INTERVIEWED HIM, FILMED HIM...

YES, ALEX. *NOW* YOU ARE THINKING LIKE A *RUSSIAN*.

"OUR INTERVIEWER ASKED HIM ABOUT A *TRAIN STRIKE* IN MOSCOW. BORIS WAS *ALREADY* HALF DRUNK, AND REPLIED:"

THIS IS MY *HOLIDAY*. I'M TOO *BUSY* TO DEAL WITH THAT.

WE WILL RELEASE FILM THAT SHOWS HIM *DRUNK* BESIDE THE SWIMMING POOL, *PLAYING* WITH HALF-NAKED GIRLS YOUNG ENOUGH TO BE HIS *DAUGHTERS*. AND THEN THE INTERVIEW...

WHAT ARE YOU GOING TO *DO* ABOUT THE ACCIDENT IN *MURMANSK*, MR PRESIDENT?

"BUT WE WILL CHANGE THE QUESTION."

THIS IS MY *HOLIDAY*. I'M TOO *BUSY* TO DEAL WITH THAT.

RUSSIA WILL *SEE* KIRIYENKO FOR THE *DRUNKEN IMBECILE* HE IS, AND BLAME *HIM*.

"THE NORTHERN FLEET WAS ONCE THE *PRIDE* OF RUSSIA! HOW COULD IT HAVE BEEN *ALLOWED* TO BECOME A RUSTING, LETHAL *NUCLEAR DUMP?*"

MANY RUSSIANS BELIEVE LIFE WAS *BETTER* IN THE OLD DAYS. THEY *HATE* WHAT RUSSIA HAS BECOME. NOW THEIR ANGER WILL BE *HEARD*. IT WILL BE *UNSTOPPABLE*.

AND I WILL *HARNESS* IT!

BEFORE THE NUCLEAR *DUST CLOUD* HAS SETTLED, I WILL HAVE *TOTAL CONTROL* OF MY COUNTRY! I WILL *REBUILD* THE BERLIN WALL! START *WARS, MANY* WARS!

I WILL NOT REST UNTIL *COMMUNIST* GOVERNMENT IS THE SINGLE *DOMINANT POWER* IN THE *WORLD!*

BUT YOU'LL KILL *MILLIONS* OF YOUR OWN PEOPLE!

PAH! MILLIONS ARE *ALREADY* DYING IN RUSSIA JUST BECAUSE THEY CANNOT AFFORD *FOOD* OR *MEDICINE!*

...

AND WHAT HAPPENS TO ME?

I'VE ALREADY *TOLD* YOU. YOU WILL BE *WITH* ME IN MOSCOW. DON'T YOU *SEE,* ALEX? YOU WILL NOT *JUST* BE MY SON. YOU WILL HAVE *POWER!*

YOU WILL BE ONE OF THE *MOST* POWERFUL PEOPLE IN THE *WORLD!*

...

TOWER TO RF-1, YOU ARE CLEARED TO LAND FOR *ROUTINE REFUELLING ONLY*. PLEASE BE PREPARED FOR *ADMINISTRATIVE BOARDING*.

ROGER, TOWER. COMMENCING *FINAL APPROACH*.

EDINBURGH, SCOTLAND, NEXT DAY

YOU WILL *NOT* SPEAK, ALEX. NOT ONE *SINGLE WORD*.

CONRAD?

IF CONRAD EVEN *THINKS* YOU ARE ABOUT TO TRY SOMETHING FOOLISH, HE WILL *FIRE*. DEATH WILL BE *INSTANT*, BUT IT WILL APPEAR AS IF YOU HAVE MERELY FALLEN *ASLEEP*.

HERE COMES THE *REFUELLING TRUCK*. REMEMBER, NOW. NOT A *SOUND*.

D'YE SPEAK *ENGLISH?* I'VE GOT SOME *PAPERS* FOR YE TO SIGN.

YES.

CHEERS. HERE'S YER *RECEIPT.* WE'LL HAVE YE BACK IN THE AIR IN *NAE* TIME AT ALL.

THANK YOU.

WILL YE NOT COME *OUT* AND STRETCH YER *LEGS?* IT'S A FINE DAY, AND WE'VE GOT *TEA* AND *SHORTBREAD* IN THE OFFICE.

NO, THANK YOU. WE ARE ALL A LITTLE *TIRED.*

ALL RIGHT, IF YE'RE SURE. *CHEERIO!*

!

SHHIDOWNN!

RELAX, CONRAD. I'M NOT *GOING* ANYWHERE. MY *LEGS* ARE A BIT *NUMB*, THAT'S ALL.

Klik - Klik - Klik

THE ONLY THING *YE'RE* DOING IS COMING WITH *ME* TO SECURITY. COME *ALONG* NOW!

AH, ALEX! *THERE* YOU ARE!

FOR GOD'S SAKE, HE'S GOT A *NUCLEAR BOMB!* HE'S GOING TO *DETONATE* IT IN *MURMANSK!* YOU *HAVE* TO LET ME CALL MI6!

WHO ARE *YE?*

I AM ALEX'S *FATHER.* ISN'T THAT *RIGHT*, ALEX?

HE'LL KILL THE GUARD IF I DENY IT...

YES ... *DAD.*

HAS ALEX MADE A *TELEPHONE CALL?*

NO. WEE RASCAL WAS HELPING HIMSELF WHEN I *CAUGHT* HIM, AND I PUT A *STOP* TAE IT.

SO WHAT'S ALL THIS BUSINESS ABOUT *BOMBS* AND *SPIES?*

DO THEY *REALLY* KEEP NUCLEAR SUBS IN *HERE*? I'VE SEEN BETTER SECURITY IN A *SUPERMARKET CAR PARK*!

EY! KTO ETO? SHTO VHI ZDES DELAYETYE?

THERE IT IS ...
THE **BASE** OF THE
NORTHERN FLEET.
WHAT A **DUMP!**

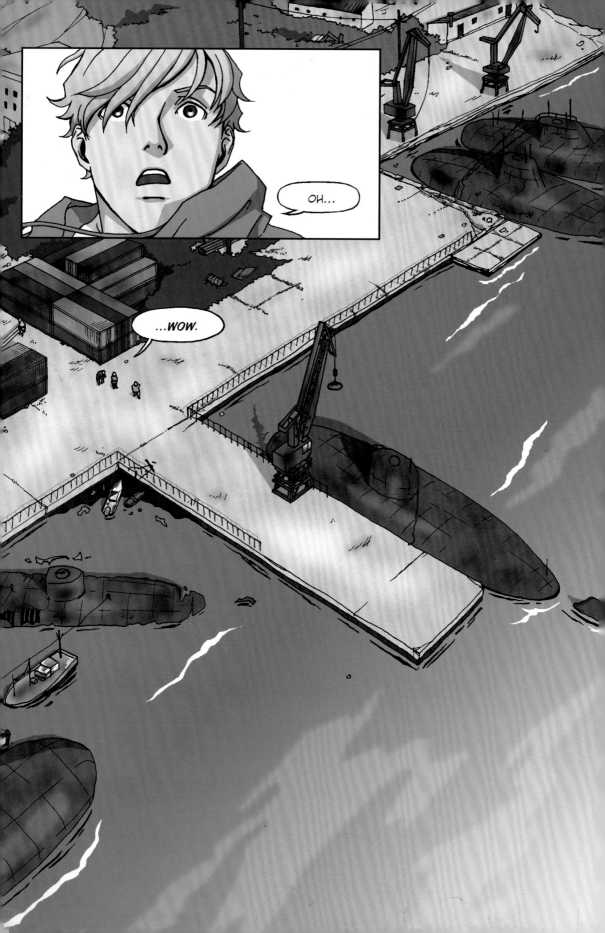

CHEW THE GUM FOR **THIRTY SECONDS**, THAT'S WHAT SMITHERS SAID...

IF SAROV COULD **SEE** THIS ... FACING DEATH, AND I'M **CHEWING**

GUM. "TYPICAL WESTERN KID"!

YUCK.

NEED TO WORK ON THAT **FLAVOUR**, SMITHERS...

...LET'S HOPE THE **OTHER** PART OF THE FORMULA WORKS BETTER.

CAN'T ... BREATHE ...
BLACKING OUT...

WAIT...

WHAT'S THAT...?

THE **DISC**...

SAROV SAID ...
METAL PINS...

ALL ... OVER ...
CONRAD'S BODY...

MMMF!

WHA...?

TOOK ME BYY
SURRRPRISE ... WON'T
DOO THAT **AGAINNN!**

I DON'T **NEED** TO.

WHAT AN *ATTRACTIVE* SIGHT.

WUPPA WUPPA WUPPA **Budda** WUPPA **Budda Budda** wuppa wuppa...

BOOM

FEELS LIKE I'VE GONE *TEN ROUNDS* WITH A *HEAVYWEIGHT.* BUT I'LL FEEL *WORSE* IF THAT BOMB GOES OFF...

THE *CONTROLS* SEEM PRETTY SIMPLE...

Zmmmmm...

GOT IT!

NOW I NEED TO DITCH THIS *EXCESS WEIGHT!*

klik

Splash!

Brakka Brakka

WOAH!

Sptang!

Sptang!

Sptang!

Budda Budda Budda

THANKS, HELICOPTER GUY!

PHEW! JUST A GRENADE GOING OFF. I THOUGHT I WAS A GONER...!

THERE'S THE CARD!

Beeeep

99:88:88

THE COUNTDOWN'S STOPPED. I DID IT!

I DID IT!

PUT IT BACK.

BLAM....

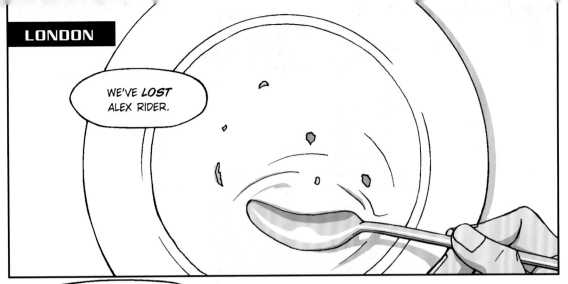

WE'VE *LOST* ALEX RIDER.

SORRY, ALAN. I KNOW IT'S *NOT* WHAT YOU WANTED TO HEAR, BUT THAT'S THE *END* OF IT.

MMM.

HE DID VERY *WELL*.

IT WOULDN'T *SURPRISE* ME IF THE CIA STARTED TRAINING THEIR *OWN* TEENAGE SPY NOW. THEY'RE *ALWAYS* COPYING OUR IDEAS.

WHEN *WE'RE* NOT COPYING *THEIRS*.

OH, YES. I HAD AN EMAIL FROM *JOE BYRNE* AT THE *CIA*. HE WAS UPSET ABOUT THE LOSS OF HIS *OWN* AGENTS, BUT HE WAS FULL OF *PRAISE* FOR ALEX.

HE DEFINITELY OWES US A *FAVOUR*.

I'VE READ THE *FILE*, BUT PERHAPS YOU CAN FILL ME IN ON THE *DETAILS*. HOW *EXACTLY* DID THE RUSSIANS FIND OUT ABOUT SAROV IN *TIME*?

BECAUSE OF WHAT HAPPENED AT *EDINBURGH AIRPORT.* ALEX *ESCAPED* FROM SAROV'S PLANE AND RAN INTO A *SECURITY GUARD.*

ALEX ACTUALLY TOLD HIM THE *TRUTH* ABOUT HIMSELF, ABOUT US, *EVERYTHING.* BUT THE GUARD DIDN'T *BELIEVE* IT.

"SAROV CAUGHT UP WITH THEM AND *SHOT* THE GUARD. ALEX MUST HAVE THOUGHT THAT WAS THE *END* OF IT...

"...BUT *LUCKILY* FOR US, THE GUARD'S *RADIO* WAS ACTIVATED THE WHOLE TIME. HIS OFFICE HEARD *EVERYTHING.*"

THEY DIDN'T BELIEVE IT *EITHER,* OF COURSE ... UNTIL THEY FOUND HIM WITH A *BULLET* IN HIS HEAD. THEN THEY CALLED *US.*

I CONTACTED MURMANSK, AND THE RUSSIANS *STORMED* THE YARD WITH A NAVAL FORCE AND GUNSHIPS.

WHAT HAPPENED TO THE *NUCLEAR BOMB?*

MMM. WHERE *IS* THE PRESIDENT?

THEY FOUND HIM *LOCKED UP* ON SKELETON KEY, SHOUTING HIS HEAD OFF AND BLAMING EVERYONE *EXCEPT* HIMSELF. HE'S BACK IN MOSCOW NOW.

THE *RUSSIANS* HAVE IT. APPARENTLY IT WAS POWERFUL ENOUGH TO *KILL* EVERYONE ON THE KOLA PENINSULA AND *CONTAMINATE* MOST OF EUROPE.

IT REALLY *WOULD* HAVE FORCED KIRIYENKO OUT OF POWER. NOBODY *LIKES* HIM MUCH ANYWAY.

AND WHAT DO THE *CUBANS* HAVE TO SAY FOR THEMSELVES?

THEY'VE *DISOWNED* SAROV. NOTHING TO DO WITH THEM, THEY HAD NO IDEA WHAT HE WAS PLANNING, *BLAH BLAH.*

RIGHT, AND *I'M* THE *PRIME MINISTER.* STILL, IF NOT FOR ALEX...

...WHO *KNOWS* WHAT MIGHT HAVE HAPPENED.

WHERE *IS* ALEX NOW?

PLEASE, ALEX, AT LEAST *TRY* TO EAT. YOU'VE HARDLY TOUCHED *ANYTHING* SINCE YOU GOT BACK.

CHELSEA, LONDON

I THINK YOU SHOULD GO SEE A *DOCTOR*. IT'S *OBVIOUS* YOU'RE NOT WELL.

NO.

I'M FINE.

WELL THEN, WHAT DO YOU WANT TO *DO* TODAY? YOU WANT TO GO CATCH A *MOVIE?*

I THINK I'LL JUST GO FOR A *WALK.*

ALL RIGHT. I'LL COME *WITH* YOU.

NO. THANKS, JACK, REALLY. BUT I'M *FINE* ON MY OWN.

Slam

SO BE IT.

GOODBYE, ALEX.

FOR EVER.

BLAM!

ALEX!

ARE YOU ALL RIGHT? I WAS SO *WORRIED*, THEY WOULDN'T TELL ME WHERE THEY *TOOK* YOU...

WHAT HAPPENED? YOU'RE *COVERED* IN BRUISES.

I CAN'T *TELL* YOU, SAB. YOU *KNOW* THAT.

WELL, IF YOU *DON'T* WANT TO TALK ABOUT IT, WHY DID YOU *TEXT* ME?

I ... I JUST WANTED TO *SEE* YOU.

I WATCHED A MAN *KILL HIMSELF* LAST WEEK. HE ... HE JUST SHOT HIMSELF, RIGHT IN *FRONT* OF ME.

AND ... IT WAS *MY FAULT.*

I DON'T **BELIEVE** THAT.

BUT IT'S **TRUE**. IT WAS ALL SO **UNREAL**...

BUT THIS WAS THE **LAST TIME**.

OH, YOU **ALWAYS** SAY THAT.

I **MEAN** IT.

I JUST WANT A **NORMAL** LIFE, SAB. AS NORMAL AS MINE **CAN** BE, ANYWAY.

DO YOU FANCY COMING TO **FRANCE**, THEN?

WHAT?

WELL, **CORNWALL** WAS RUINED, WASN'T IT? BUT MY **PARENTS** ARE TAKING ME TO THE SOUTH OF FRANCE NEXT MONTH, SO I WANT **YOU** TO COME **WITH** US.

First published 2009 by Walker Books Ltd
87 Vauxhall Walk, London SE11 5HJ

This edition published 2012

2 4 6 8 10 9 7 5 3 1

Text and illustrations © 2009 Walker Books Ltd
Based on the original novel *Skeleton Key* © 2002 Stormbreaker Productions Ltd

Anthony Horowitz has asserted his moral rights.

Trademarks © 2002 Stormbreaker Productions Ltd
Alex Rider™, Boy with Torch Logo™, AR Logo™

This book has been typeset in Wild Words and Serpentine Bold

Printed in China

British Library Cataloguing in Publication Data:
a catalogue record for this book is available from the British Library

ISBN 978-1-4063-4093-8

www.walker.co.uk

ANTHONY HOROWITZ (BA/Nielsen Author of the Year) is one of the most popular children's writers working today. His hugely successful Alex Rider series has sold over ten million copies worldwide and won numerous awards, including the Children's Book of the Year Award for ARK ANGEL at the British Book Awards and the Red House Children's Book Award for SKELETON KEY. He scripted the blockbuster movie STORMBREAKER from his own novel, and also writes extensively for TV, with programmes including MIDSOMER MURDERS, COLLISION, INJUSTICE and FOYLE'S WAR. Anthony Horowitz is the author of THE HOUSE OF SILK: THE NEW SHERLOCK HOLMES NOVEL. He is married to television producer Jill Green and lives in Clerkenwell with his two sons, Nicholas and Cassian, and the ghost of their dog, Lucky.

www.anthonyhorowitz.com

ANTONY JOHNSTON, who wrote the script for this book, is a veteran author of comics and graphic novels, from superheroes such as DAREDEVIL and WOLVERINE, to science-fiction adventures like WASTELAND and DEAD SPACE, and even thrillers such as THE COLDEST CITY and JULIUS. He also writes videogames, including many of the DEAD SPACE series, and other games like BINARY DOMAIN and XCOM. His debut fiction novel FRIGHTENING CURVES won an IPPY award for Best Horror. Antony lives in North-West England with his partner Marcia, his dogs Connor and Rosie, and far too many gadgets with apples printed on them.

www.antonyjohnston.com

The artwork in this graphic novel is the work of two artists, **KANAKO DAMERUM** and **YUZURU TAKASAKI**, who collaborate on every illustration. Although living on opposite sides of the globe, these Japanese sisters work seamlessly together via the Internet.

Living and working in Tokyo, **YUZURU** produced all the line work for these illustrations using traditional means. The quality of her draughtsmanship comes from years of honing her skills in the highly competitive world of manga.

KANAKO lives and works out of her studio in London. She managed and directed the project as well as colouring and rendering the artwork digitally using her wealth of knowledge in graphic design.

www.manga-media.com
www.thorogood.net

Collect all the Alex Rider books

ALEX RIDER MISSION 1 : STORMBREAKER
ANTHONY HOROWITZ

ALEX RIDER MISSION 2 : POINT BLANC
ANTHONY HOROWITZ

ALEX RIDER MISSION 3 : SKELETON KEY
ANTHONY HOROWITZ

ALEX RIDER MISSION 4 : EAGLE STRIKE
ANTHONY HOROWITZ

ALEX RIDER MISSION 5 : SCORPIA
ANTHONY HOROWITZ

ALEX RIDER MISSION 6 : ARK ANGEL
ANTHONY HOROWITZ

ALEX RIDER MISSION 7 : SNAKEHEAD
ANTHONY HOROWITZ

ALEX RIDER MISSION 8 : CROCODILE TEARS
ANTHONY HOROWITZ

ALEX RIDER MISSION 9 : SCORPIA RISING
ANTHONY HOROWITZ

and the graphic novels

ALEX RIDER
ANTHONY HOROWITZ
ANTONY JOHNSTON
KANAKO AND YUZURU
THE GRAPHIC NOVEL
STORMBREAKER

ALEX RIDER
ANTHONY HOROWITZ
ANTONY JOHNSTON
KANAKO AND YUZURU
THE GRAPHIC NOVEL
POINT BLANC

ALEX RIDER
ANTHONY HOROWITZ
ANTONY JOHNSTON
KANAKO AND YUZURU
THE GRAPHIC NOVEL
EAGLE STRIKE

alexrider.com